TAO
TE
CHING

PHOTOGRAPHY BY JANE ENGLISH

CALLIGRAPHY BY GIA-FU FENG

# LAO TSU  TAO TE CHING

A NEW TRANSLATION BY GIA-FU FENG AND JANE ENGLISH

Gower

First published in Great Britain by
Wildwood House Ltd
Reprinted 1973, 1974 (twice), 1975, 1976, 1984, 1986, 1988, 1991, 1992, 1993

This edition reprinted 1996 by
Gower Publishing
Gower House
Croft Road
Aldershot
Hampshire GU11 3HR
England

ISBN 0 7045 0007 8

Printed and bound in Great Britain by
Woolnough Bookbinding Ltd, Irthlingborough, Northamptonshire

## LAO TSU AND TAOISM

Lao Tsu, an older contemporary of Confucius, was keeper of the imperial archives at Loyang in the province of Honan in the sixth century B.C. All his life he taught that "The Tao that can be told is not the eternal Tao"; but, according to ancient legend, as he was riding off into the desert to die—sick at heart at the ways of men—he was persuaded by a gatekeeper in northwestern China to write down his teaching for posterity.

The essence of Taoism is contained in the eighty-one chapters of the book—roughly 5,000 words— which have for 2,500 years provided one of the major underlying influences in Chinese thought and culture, emerging also in proverbs and folklore. Whereas Confucianism is concerned with day-to-day rules of conduct, Taoism is concerned with a more spiritual level of being.

# TAO
# TE
# CHING

道可道非常道名可名非常名無名天地之始

有名萬物之母故常無欲以觀其妙

常有欲以觀其徼此兩者同出而異名

同謂之元元之又元眾妙之門

## ONE

The Tao that can be told is not the eternal Tao.
The name that can be named is not the eternal name.
The nameless is the beginning of heaven and earth.
The named is the mother of ten thousand things.
Ever desireless, one can see the mystery.
Ever desiring, one can see the manifestations.
These two spring from the same source but differ in name;
    this appears as darkness.
Darkness within darkness.
The gate to all mystery.

TWO

Under heaven all can see beauty as beauty only because there is ugliness.
All can know good as good only because there is evil.

Therefore having and not having arise together.
Difficult and easy complement each other.
Long and short contrast each other;
High and low rest upon each other;
Voice and sound harmonize each other;
Front and back follow one another.

Therefore the sage goes about doing nothing, teaching no-talking.
The ten thousand things rise and fall without cease,
Creating, yet not possessing,
Working, yet not taking credit.
Work is done, then forgotten.
Therefore it lasts forever.

天下皆知美之為美斯惡已皆知善之為善斯不善已

故有無相生難易相成長短相較高下相傾音聲相和前後相隨

是以聖人處無為之事行不言之教萬物作焉而不辭

生而不有為而不恃功成而弗居

夫唯弗居是以不去

不尚賢使民不爭不貴難得之貨使民不為盜

不見可欲使民心不亂

是以聖人之治虛其心實其腹弱其志強其骨

常使民無知無欲使夫智者不敢為也為無為則無不治

THREE

Not exalting the gifted prevents quarreling.
Not collecting treasures prevents stealing.
Not seeing desirable things prevents confusion of the heart.

The wise therefore rule by emptying hearts and stuffing bellies,
    by weakening ambitions and strengthening bones.
If people lack knowledge and desire,
    then intellectuals will not try to interfere.
If nothing is done, then all will be well.

道沖而用之或不盈淵兮似萬物之宗挫其銳

解其紛和其光同其塵湛兮似或存

吾不知誰之子象帝之先

FOUR

The Tao is an empty vessel; it is used, but never filled.
Oh, unfathomable source of ten thousand things!
Blunt the sharpness,
Untangle the knot,
Soften the glare,
Merge with dust.
Oh, hidden deep but ever present!
I do not know from whence it comes.
It is the forefather of the emperors.

天地不仁以萬物為芻狗聖人不仁以百姓為芻狗

天地之間其猶橐籥乎虛而不屈動而愈出

多言數窮不如守中

FIVE

Heaven and earth are ruthless;
They see the ten thousand things as dummies.
The wise are ruthless;
They see the people as dummies.

The space between heaven and earth is like a bellows.
The shape changes but not the form;
The more it moves, the more it yields.
More words count less.
Hold fast to the center.

谷神不死是謂元牝元牝之門是謂天地根

緜緜若存用之不勤

SIX

The valley spirit never dies;
It is the woman, primal mother.
Her gateway is the root of heaven and earth.
It is like a veil barely seen.
Use it; it will never fail.

天長地久天地所以能長且久者以其不自生

故能長生是以聖人後其身而身先外其身而身存

非以其無私邪故能成其私

SEVEN

Heaven and earth last forever.
Why do heaven and earth last forever?
They are unborn,
So ever living.
The sage stays behind, thus he is ahead.
He is detached, thus at one with all.
Through selfless action, he attains fulfillment.

上善若水水善利萬物而不爭處眾人之所惡

故幾於道居善地心善淵與善仁言善信正善治

事善能動善時夫唯不爭故無尤

EIGHT

The highest good is like water.
Water gives life to the ten thousand things and does not strive.
It flows in places men reject and so is like the Tao.

In dwelling, be close to the land.
In meditation, go deep in the heart.
In dealing with others, be gentle and kind.
In speech, be true.
In ruling, be just.
In business, be competent.
In action, watch the timing.

No fight: No blame.

持而盈之不如其已揣而梲之不可長保

金玉滿堂莫之能守富貴而驕自遺其咎

功遂身退天之道

NINE

Better stop short than fill to the brim.
Oversharpen the blade, and the edge will soon blunt.
Amass a store of gold and jade, and no one can protect it.
Claim wealth and titles, and disaster will follow.
Retire when the work is done.
This is the way of heaven.

載營魄抱一能無離乎專氣致柔能嬰兒乎

滌除元覽能無疵乎愛民治國能無知乎

天門開闔能無雌乎明白四達能無為乎

生之畜之生而不有為而不恃

長而不宰是謂元德

## TEN

Carrying body and soul and embracing the one,
Can you avoid separation?
Attending fully and becoming supple,
Can you be as a newborn babe?
Washing and cleansing the primal vision,
Can you be without stain?
Loving all men and ruling the country,
Can you be without cleverness?
Opening and closing the gates of heaven,
Can you play the role of woman?
Understanding and being open to all things,
Are you able to do nothing?
Giving birth and nourishing,
Bearing yet not possessing,
Working yet not taking credit,
Leading yet not dominating,
This is the Primal Virtue.

三十輻共一轂當其無有車之用

埏埴以為器當其無有器之用

鑿戶牖以為室當其無有室之用

故有之以為利無之以為用

ELEVEN

Thirty spokes share the wheel's hub;
It is the center hole that makes it useful.
Shape clay into a vessel;
It is the space within that makes it useful.
Cut doors and windows for a room;
It is the holes which make it useful.
Therefore profit comes from what is there;
Usefulness from what is not there.

TWELVE

The five colors blind the eye.
The five tones deafen the ear.
The five flavors dull the taste.
Racing and hunting madden the mind.
Precious things lead one astray.

Therefore the sage is guided by what he feels and not by what he sees.
He lets go of that and chooses this.

五色令人目盲五音令人耳聾五味令人口爽

馳騁畋獵令人心發狂難得之貨令人行妨

是以聖人為腹不為目

故去彼取此

寵辱若驚貴大患若身

何謂寵辱若敬驚寵為下得之若驚失之若驚是謂寵辱若驚

何謂貴大患若身吾所以有大患者為吾有身及吾無身吾有何患

故貴以身為天下若可寄天下愛以身為天下若可託天下

# THIRTEEN

Accept disgrace willingly.
Accept misfortune as the human condition.

What do you mean by "Accept disgrace willingly"?
Accept being unimportant.
Do not be concerned with loss or gain.
This is called "accepting disgrace willingly."

What do you mean by "Accept misfortune as the human condition"?
Misfortune comes from having a body.
Without a body, how could there be misfortune?

Surrender yourself humbly; then you can be trusted to care for all things.
Love the world as your own self; then you can truly care for all things.

## FOURTEEN

Look, it cannot be seen—it is beyond form.
Listen, it cannot be heard—it is beyond sound.
Grasp, it cannot be held—it is intangible.
These three are indefinable;
Therefore they are joined in one.

From above it is not bright;
From below it is not dark:
An unbroken thread beyond description.
It returns to nothingness.
The form of the formless,
The image of the imageless,
It is called indefinable and beyond imagination.

Stand before it and there is no beginning.
Follow it and there is no end.
Stay with the ancient Tao,
Move with the present.

Knowing the ancient beginning is the essence of Tao.

視之不見名曰夷聽之不聞名曰希搏之不得名曰微

此三者不可致詰故混而為一其上不皦其下不昧

繩繩不可名復歸於無物是謂無狀之狀無物之象是謂惚恍

迎之不見其首隨之不見其後

執古之道以御今之有能知古始是謂道紀

古之善為士者微妙玄通深不可識

夫唯不可識故強為之容

豫焉若冬涉川猶兮若畏四鄰儼兮其若容

渙兮若冰之將釋敦兮其若樸曠兮其若谷

混兮其若濁孰能濁以靜之徐清孰能安以久動之徐生

保此道者不欲盈夫唯不盈故能蔽不新成

FIFTEEN

The ancient masters were subtle, mysterious, profound, responsive.
The depth of their knowledge is unfathomable.
Because it is unfathomable,
All we can do is describe their appearance.
Watchful, like men crossing a winter stream.
Alert, like men aware of danger.
Courteous, like visiting guests.
Yielding, like ice about to melt.
Simple, like uncarved blocks of wood.
Hollow, like caves.
Opaque, like muddy pools.

Who can wait quietly while the mud settles?
Who can remain still until the moment of action?
Observers of the Tao do not seek fulfillment.
Not seeking fulfillment, they are not swayed by desire for change.

致虛極守靜篤萬物並作吾以觀復夫物芸芸各復歸其根

歸根曰靜是謂復命復命曰常知常曰明

不知常妄作凶知常容容乃公公乃王

王乃天天乃道道乃久沒身不殆

SIXTEEN

Empty yourself of everything.
Let the mind rest at peace.
The ten thousand things rise and fall while the Self watches their return.
They grow and flourish and then return to the source.
Returning to the source is stillness, which is the way of nature.
The way of nature is unchanging.
Knowing constancy is insight.
Not knowing constancy leads to disaster.
Knowing constancy, the mind is open.
With an open mind, you will be openhearted.
Being openhearted, you will act royally.
Being royal, you will attain the divine.
Being divine, you will be at one with the Tao.
Being at one with the Tao is eternal.
And though the body dies, the Tao will never pass away.

SEVENTEEN

The very highest is barely known by men.
Then comes that which they know and love,
Then that which is feared,
Then that which is despised.

He who does not trust enough will not be trusted.

When actions are performed
Without unnecessary speech,
People say, "We did it!"

太上下知有之其次親而譽之

其次畏之其次侮之

信不足焉有不信焉

悠兮其貴言功成事遂百姓皆謂我自然

大道廢有仁義慧智出有大偽
六親不和有孝慈國家昏亂有忠臣

EIGHTEEN

When the great Tao is forgotten,
Kindness and morality arise.
When wisdom and intelligence are born,
The great pretense begins.

When there is no peace within the family,
Filial piety and devotion arise.
When the country is confused and in chaos,
Loyal ministers appear.

絶聖棄智民利百倍

絶仁棄義民復孝慈絶巧棄利盜賊無有

此三者以為文不足故令有所屬見素抱樸少私寡欲

NINETEEN

Give up sainthood, renounce wisdom,
And it will be a hundred times better for everyone.

Give up kindness, renounce morality,
And men will rediscover filial piety and love.

Give up ingenuity, renounce profit,
And bandits and thieves will disappear.

These three are outward forms alone; they are not sufficient in themselves.
It is more important
To see the simplicity,
To realize one's true nature,
To cast off selfishness
And temper desire.

絕學無憂唯之與阿相去幾何善之與惡相去若何

人之所畏不可不畏荒兮其未央哉

眾人熙熙如享太牢如春登臺我獨泊兮其未兆

如嬰兒之未孩儽儽兮若無所歸眾人皆有餘而我獨若遺

我愚人之心也哉沌沌兮俗人昭昭我獨昏昏

俗人察察我獨悶悶澹兮其若海飂兮若無止

眾人皆有以而我獨頑似鄙我獨異於人而貴食母

TWENTY

Give up learning, and put an end to your troubles.

Is there a difference between yes and no?
Is there a difference between good and evil?
Must I fear what others fear? What nonsense!
Other people are contented, enjoying the sacrificial feast of the ox.
In spring some go to the park, and climb the terrace,
But I alone am drifting, not knowing where I am.
Like a newborn babe before it learns to smile,
I am alone, without a place to go.

Others have more than they need, but I alone have nothing.
I am a fool. Oh, yes! I am confused.
Other men are clear and bright,
But I alone am dim and weak.
Other men are sharp and clever,
But I alone am dull and stupid.
Oh, I drift like the waves of the sea,
Without direction, like the restless wind.

Everyone else is busy,
But I alone am aimless and depressed.
I am different.
I am nourished by the great mother.

孔德之容惟道是從道之為物惟恍惟惚
惚兮恍兮其中有象恍兮惚兮其中有物
窈兮冥兮其中有精其精甚真其中有信
自古及今其名不去以閱眾甫
吾何以知眾甫之狀哉以此

TWENTY-ONE

The greatest Virtue is to follow Tao and Tao alone.
The Tao is elusive and intangible.
Oh, it is intangible and elusive, and yet within is image.
Oh, it is elusive and intangible, and yet within is form.
Oh, it is dim and dark, and yet within is essence.
This essence is very real, and therein lies faith.
From the very beginning until now its name has never been forgotten.
Thus I perceive the creation.
How do I know the ways of creation?
Because of this.

曲則全枉則直窪則盈敝則新少則得多則惑

是以聖人抱一為天下式不自見故明不自是故彰不自伐故有功

不自矜故長夫唯不爭故天下莫能與之爭

古之所謂曲則全者豈虛言哉誠全而歸之

TWENTY-TWO

Yield and overcome;
Bend and be straight;
Empty and be full;
Wear out and be new;
Have little and gain;
Have much and be confused.

Therefore wise men embrace the one
And set an example to all.
Not putting on a display,
They shine forth.
Not justifying themselves,
They are distinguished.
Not boasting,
They receive recognition.
Not bragging,
They never falter.
They do not quarrel,
So no one quarrels with them.
Therefore the ancients say, "Yield and overcome."
Is that an empty saying?
Be really whole,
And all things will come to you.

## TWENTY-THREE

To talk little is natural.
High winds do not last all morning.
Heavy rain does not last all day.
Why is this? Heaven and earth!
If heaven and earth cannot make things eternal,
How is it possible for man?

He who follows the Tao
Is at one with the Tao.
He who is virtuous
Experiences Virtue.
He who loses the way
Feels lost.
When you are at one with the Tao,
The Tao welcomes you.
When you are at one with Virtue,
The Virtue is always there.
When you are at one with loss,
The loss is experienced willingly.

He who does not trust enough
Will not be trusted.

希言自然故飄風不終朝驟雨不終日孰為此者天地

天地尚不能久而況於人乎

故從事於道者道同於道德者同於德失者同於失

同於道者道亦樂得之同於德者德亦樂得之

同於失者失亦樂得之信不足焉有不信焉

企者不立跨者不行自見者不明
自是者不彰自伐者無功
自矜者不長其在道也曰
餘食贅行物或惡之故有道者不處

## TWENTY-FOUR

He who stands on tiptoe is not steady.
He who strides cannot maintain the pace.
He who makes a show is not enlightened.
He who is self-righteous is not respected.
He who boasts achieves nothing.
He who brags will not endure.
According to followers of the Tao,
    "These are extra food and unnecessary luggage."
They do not bring happiness.
Therefore followers of the Tao avoid them.

有物混成先天地生
寂兮寥兮獨立不改周行而不殆可以為天下母
吾不知其名字之曰道強為之名曰大
大曰逝逝曰遠遠曰反
故道大天大地大王亦大
域中有四大而王居其一焉人法地地法天天法道道法自然

## TWENTY-FIVE

Something mysteriously formed,
Born before heaven and earth.
In the silence and the void,
Standing alone and unchanging,
Ever present and in motion.
Perhaps it is the mother of ten thousand things.
I do not know its name.
Call it Tao.
For lack of a better word, I call it great.

Being great, it flows.
It flows far away.
Having gone far, it returns.

Therefore, "Tao is great;
Heaven is great;
Earth is great;
The king is also great."
These are the four great powers
    of the universe,
And the king is one of them.

Man follows the earth.
Earth follows heaven.
Heaven follows the Tao.
Tao follows what is natural.

重為輕根靜為躁君

是以聖人終日行不離輜重雖有榮觀燕處超然

奈何萬乘之主而以身輕天下輕則失本躁則失君

## TWENTY-SIX

The heavy is the root of the light;
The still is the master of unrest.

Therefore the sage, traveling all day,
Does not lose sight of his baggage.
Though there are beautiful things to be seen,
He remains unattached and calm.

Why should the lord of ten thousand chariots act lightly in public?
To be light is to lose one's root.
To be restless is to lose one's control.

TWENTY-SEVEN

A good walker leaves no tracks;
A good speaker makes no slips;
A good reckoner needs no tally.
A good door needs no lock,
Yet no one can open it.
Good binding requires no knots,
Yet no one can loosen it.

Therefore the sage takes care of all men
And abandons no one.
He takes care of all things
And abandons nothing.

This is called "following the light."

What is a good man?
A teacher of a bad man.
What is a bad man?
A good man's charge.
If the teacher is not respected,
And the student not cared for,
Confusion will arise, however clever one is.
This is the crux of mystery.

善行無轍迹　善言無瑕謫　善數不用籌策
善閉無關楗而不可開　善結無繩約而不可解
是以聖人常善救人　故無棄人　常善救物　故無棄物
是謂襲明　故善人者　不善人之師
不善人者　善人之資　不貴其師
不愛其資　雖智大迷　是謂要妙

知其雄守其雌為天下谿為天下谿常德不離復歸於嬰兒

知其白守其黑為天下式為天下式常德不忒復歸於無極

知其榮守其辱為天下谷為天下谷常德乃足復歸於樸

樸散則為器聖人用之則為官長故大制不割

## TWENTY-EIGHT

Know the strength of man,
But keep a woman's care!
Be the stream of the universe!
Being the stream of the universe,
Ever true and unswerving,
Become as a little child once more.

Know the white,
But keep the black!
Be an example to the world!
Being an example to the world,
Ever true and unwavering,
Return to the infinite.

Know honor,
Yet keep humility.
Be the valley of the universe!
Being the valley of the universe,
Ever true and resourceful,
Return to the state of the uncarved block.

When the block is carved, it becomes useful.
When the sage uses it, he becomes the ruler.
Thus, "A great tailor cuts little."

## TWENTY-NINE

Do you think you can take over the universe and improve it?
I do not believe it can be done.

The universe is sacred.
You cannot improve it.
If you try to change it, you will ruin it.
If you try to hold it, you will lose it.

So sometimes things are ahead and sometimes they are behind;
Sometimes breathing is hard, sometimes it comes easily;
Sometimes there is strength and sometimes weakness;
Sometimes one is up and sometimes down.

Therefore the sage avoids extremes, excesses, and complacency.

將欲取天下而為之吾見其不得已

天下神器不可為也為者敗之執者失之

故物或行或隨或歔或吹或強或羸或挫或隳

是以聖人去甚去奢去泰

以道佐人主者不以兵強天下其事好還

師之所處荊棘生焉大軍之後必有凶年善有果而已不敢以取強

果而勿矜果而勿伐果而勿驕果而不得已果而勿強

物壯則老是謂不道不道早已

THIRTY

Whenever you advise a ruler in the way of Tao,
Counsel him not to use force to conquer the universe.
For this would only cause resistance.
Thorn bushes spring up wherever the army has passed.
Lean years follow in the wake of a great war.
Just do what needs to be done.
Never take advantage of power.

Achieve results,
But never glory in them.
Achieve results,
But never boast.
Achieve results,
But never be proud.
Achieve results,
Because this is the natural way.
Achieve results,
But not through violence.

Force is followed by loss of strength.
This is not the way of Tao.
That which goes against the Tao
    comes to an early end.

夫佳兵者不祥之器物或惡之故有道者不處

君子居則貴左用兵則貴右兵者不祥之器非君子之器

不得已而用之恬淡為上勝而不美而美之者是樂殺人

夫樂殺人者則不可得志於天下矣吉事尚左凶事尚右

偏將軍居左上將軍居右言以喪禮處之

殺人之眾以哀悲泣之戰勝以喪禮處之

THIRTY-ONE

Good weapons are instruments of fear; all creatures hate them.
Therefore followers of Tao never use them.
The wise man prefers the left.
The man of war prefers the right.

Weapons are instruments of fear; they are not a wise man's tools.
He uses them only when he has no choice.
Peace and quiet are dear to his heart,
And victory no cause for rejoicing.
If you rejoice in victory, then you delight in killing;
If you delight in killing, you cannot fulfill yourself.

On happy occasions precedence is given to the left,
On sad occasions to the right.
In the army the general stands on the left,
The commander-in-chief on the right.
This means that war is conducted like a funeral.
When many people are being killed,
They should be mourned in heartfelt sorrow.
That is why a victory must be observed like a funeral.

道常無名樸雖小天下莫能臣也侯王若能守之萬物將自賓

天地相合以降甘露民莫之令而自均

始制有名名亦既有夫亦將知止知止可以不殆

譬道之在天下猶川谷之於江海

## THIRTY-TWO

The Tao is forever undefined.
Small though it is in the unformed state, it cannot be grasped.
If kings and lords could harness it,
The ten thousand things would naturally obey.
Heaven and earth would come together
And gentle rain fall.
Men would need no more instruction
    and all things would take their course.

Once the whole is divided, the parts need names.
There are already enough names.
One must know when to stop.
Knowing when to stop averts trouble.
Tao in the world is like a river flowing home to the sea.

知人者智　自知者明　勝人者有力　自勝者強

知足者富　強行者有志　不失其所者久　死而不亡者壽

THIRTY-THREE

Knowing others is wisdom;
Knowing the self is enlightenment.
Mastering others requires force;
Mastering the self needs strength.

He who knows he has enough is rich.
Perseverance is a sign of will power.
He who stays where he is endures.
To die but not to perish is to be eternally present.

大道氾兮其可左右万物恃之而生而不辭功成而不名有
衣養万物而不為主常無欲可名於小
万物歸焉而不為主可名為大
以其終不自為大故能成其大

## THIRTY-FOUR

The great Tao flows everywhere, both to the left and to the right.
The ten thousand things depend upon it; it holds nothing back.
It fulfills its purpose silently and makes no claim.

It nourishes the ten thousand things,
And yet is not their lord.
It has no aim; it is very small.

The ten thousand things return to it,
Yet it is not their lord.
It is very great.

It does not show greatness,
And is therefore truly great.

執大象，天下往，往而不害，安平太。樂與餌，過客止。

道之出口，淡乎其無味，視之不足見，聽之不足聞，用之不足既。

## THIRTY-FIVE

All men will come to him who keeps to the one,
For there lie rest and happiness and peace.

Passersby may stop for music and good food,
But a description of the Tao
Seems without substance or flavor.
It cannot be seen, it cannot be heard,
And yet it cannot be exhausted.

THIRTY-SIX

That which shrinks
Must first expand.
That which fails
Must first be strong.
That which is cast down
Must first be raised.
Before receiving
There must be giving.

This is called perception of the nature of things.
Soft and weak overcome hard and strong.

Fish cannot leave deep waters,
And a country's weapons should not be displayed.

将欲歙之必固張之將欲弱之必固強之
將欲廢之必固興之將欲奪之必固與之
是謂微明柔弱勝剛強魚不可脫於淵
國之利器不可以示人

道常無為而無不為侯王若能守之

萬物將自化化而欲作吾將鎮之以無名之樸

無名之樸夫亦將無欲不欲以靜天下將自定

THIRTY-SEVEN

Tao abides in non-action,
Yet nothing is left undone.
If kings and lords observed this,
The ten thousand things would develop naturally.
If they still desired to act,
They would return to the simplicity of formless substance.
Without form there is no desire.
Without desire there is tranquillity.
And in this way all things would be at peace.

上德不德是以有德下德不失德是以無德
上德無為而無以為下德為之而有以為
上仁為之而無以為上義為之而有以為上禮為之而莫之應則攘臂而扔之
故失道而後德失德而後仁失仁而後義失義而後禮夫禮者忠信之薄而亂之首
前識者道之華而愚之始是以大丈夫處其厚不居其薄處其實不居其華
故去彼取此

THIRTY-EIGHT

A truly good man is not aware of his goodness,
And is therefore good.
A foolish man tries to be good,
And is therefore not good.

A truly good man does nothing,
Yet leaves nothing undone.
A foolish man is always doing,
Yet much remains to be done.

When a truly kind man does something, he leaves nothing undone.
When a just man does something, he leaves a great deal to be done.
When a disciplinarian does something and no one responds,
He rolls up his sleeves in an attempt to enforce order.

Therefore when Tao is lost, there is goodness.
When goodness is lost, there is kindness.
When kindness is lost, there is justice.
When justice is lost, there is ritual.
Now ritual is the husk of faith and loyalty, the beginning of confusion.
Knowledge of the future is only a flowery trapping of Tao.
It is the beginning of folly.

Therefore the truly great man dwells on what is real
        and not what is on the surface,
On the fruit and not the flower.
Therefore accept the one and reject the other.

昔之得一者天得一以清地得一以寧神得一以靈谷得一以盈萬物得一以生侯王得一以為天下貞

其致之天無以清將恐裂地無以寧將恐發神無以靈將恐歇谷無以盈將恐竭

萬物無以生將恐滅侯王無以貴高將恐蹶故貴以賤為本高以下為基

是以侯王自謂孤寡不穀此非以賤為本邪非乎故致數輿無輿不欲琭琭如玉珞珞如石

THIRTY-NINE

These things from ancient times arise from one:
The sky is whole and clear.
The earth is whole and firm.
The spirit is whole and strong.
The valley is whole and full.
The ten thousand things are whole and alive.
Kings and lords are whole, and the country is upright.
All these are in virtue of wholeness.

The clarity of the sky prevents its falling.
The firmness of the earth prevents its splitting.
The strength of the spirit prevents its being used up.
The fullness of the valley prevents its running dry.
The growth of the ten thousand things prevents their dying out.
The leadership of kings and lords prevents the downfall
    of the country.

Therefore the humble is the root of the noble.
The low is the foundation of the high.
Princes and lords consider themselves
    "orphaned," "widowed," and "worthless."
Do they not depend on being humble?

Too much success is not an advantage.
Do not tinkle like jade
Or clatter like stone chimes.

FORTY

Returning is the motion of the Tao.
Yielding is the way of the Tao.
The ten thousand things are born of being.
Being is born of not being.

反者道之動弱者道之用

天下萬物生於有有生於無

FORTY-ONE

The wise student hears of the Tao and practices it diligently.
The average student hears of the Tao and gives it thought now and again.
The foolish student hears of the Tao and laughs aloud.
If there were no laughter, the Tao would not be what it is.

Hence it is said:
The bright path seems dim;
Going forward seems like retreat;
The easy way seems hard;
The highest Virtue seems empty;
Great purity seems sullied;
A wealth of Virtue seems inadequate;
The strength of Virtue seems frail;
Real Virtue seems unreal;
The perfect square has no corners;
Great talents ripen late;
The highest notes are hard to hear;
The greatest form has no shape.
The Tao is hidden and without name.
The Tao alone nourishes and brings everything to fulfillment.

上士聞道勤而行之中士聞道若存若亡下士聞道大笑之不笑不足以為道

故建言有之明道若昧進道若退夷道若纇上德若谷

大白若辱廣德若不足建德若偷質真若渝

大方無隅大器晚成大音希聲大象無形

道隱無名夫唯道善貸且成

道生一一生二二生三三生萬物負陰而抱陽冲氣以為和

人之所惡唯孤寡不穀而王公以為稱故物或損之而益或益之而損

人之所教我亦教之強梁者不得其死吾將以為教父

## FORTY-TWO

The Tao begot one.
One begot two.
Two begot three.
And three begot the ten thousand things.

The ten thousand things carry yin and embrance yang.
They achieve harmony by combining these forces.

Men hate to be "orphaned," "widowed," or "worthless,"
But this is how kings and lords describe themselves.

For one gains by losing
And loses by gaining.

What others teach, I also teach; that is:
"A violent man will die a violent death!"
This will be the essence of my teaching.

FORTY-THREE

The softest thing in the universe
Overcomes the hardest thing in the universe.
That without substance can enter where there is no room.
Hence I know the value of non-action.

Teaching without words and work without doing
Are understood by very few.

天下之至柔馳騁天下之至堅無有入於無間

吾是以知無為之有益

不言之教無為之益天下希及之

名與身孰親身與貨孰多得與亡孰病

是故甚愛必大費多藏必厚亡

知足不辱知止不殆可以長久

FORTY-FOUR

Fame or self: Which matters more?
Self or wealth: Which is more precious?
Gain or loss: Which is more painful?

He who is attached to things will suffer much.
He who saves will suffer heavy loss.
A contented man is never disappointed.
He who knows when to stop does not find himself in trouble.
He will stay forever safe.

FORTY-FIVE

Great accomplishment seems imperfect,
Yet it does not outlive its usefulness.
Great fullness seems empty,
Yet it cannot be exhausted.

Great straightness seems twisted.
Great intelligence seems stupid.
Great eloquence seems awkward.

Movement overcomes cold.
Stillness overcomes heat.
Stillness and tranquillity set things in order in the universe.

大成若缺其用不敝大盈若沖其用不窮

大直若屈大巧若拙大辯若訥

躁勝寒靜勝熱清靜為天下正

天下有道卻走馬以糞天下無道戎馬生於郊
禍莫大於不知足咎莫大於欲得故知足之足常足矣

FORTY-SIX

When the Tao is present in the universe,
The horses haul manure.
When the Tao is absent from the universe,
War horses are bred outside the city.

There is no greater sin than desire,
No greater curse than discontent,
No greater misfortune than wanting something for oneself.
Therefore he who knows that enough is enough will always have enough.

不出戶知天下不闚牖見天道其出彌遠其知彌少

是以聖人不行而知不見而名不為而成

FORTY-SEVEN

Without going outside, you may know the whole world.
Without looking through the window, you may see the ways of heaven.
The farther you go, the less you know.

Thus the sage knows without traveling;
He sees without looking;
He works without doing.

為學日益為道日損

損之又損以至於無為無不為

取天下常以無事及其有事不足以取天下

FORTY-EIGHT

In the pursuit of learning, every day something is acquired.
In the pursuit of Tao, every day something is dropped.

Less and less is done
Until non-action is achieved.
When nothing is done, nothing is left undone.

The world is ruled by letting things take their course.
It cannot be ruled by interfering.

FORTY-NINE

The sage has no mind of his own.
He is aware of the needs of others.

I am good to people who are good.
I am also good to people who are not good.
Because Virtue is goodness.
I have faith in people who are faithful.
I also have faith in people who are not faithful.
Because Virtue is faithfulness.

The sage is shy and humble—to the world he seems confusing.
Men look to him and listen.
He behaves like a little child.

聖人無常心以百姓心為心善者吾善之不善者吾亦善之德善

信者吾信之不信者吾亦信之德信

聖人在天下歙歙為天下渾其心

百姓皆注其耳目聖人皆孩之

FIFTY

Between birth and death,
Three in ten are followers of life,
Three in ten are followers of death,
And men just passing from birth to death also number three in ten.
Why is this so?
Because they live their lives on the gross level.

He who knows how to live can walk abroad
Without fear of rhinoceros or tiger.
He will not be wounded in battle.
For in him rhinoceroses can find no place to thrust their horn,
Tigers no place to use their claws,
And weapons no place to pierce.
Why is this so?
Because he has no place for death to enter.

出生入死生之徒十有三死之徒十有三人之生動之死地亦十有三

夫何故以生生之厚

蓋聞善攝生者陸行不遇兕虎入軍不被甲兵

兕無所投其角虎無所措其爪兵無所容其刃

夫何故以其無死地

道生之德畜之物形之勢成之

是以万物莫不尊道而貴德

道之尊德之貴夫莫之命而常自然

故道生之德畜之長之育之亭之毒之養之覆之

生而不有為而不恃長而不宰是謂元德

FIFTY-ONE

All things arise from Tao.
They are nourished by Virtue.
They are formed from matter.
They are shaped by environment.
Thus the ten thousand things all respect Tao and honor Virtue.
Respect of Tao and honor of Virtue are not demanded,
But they are in the nature of things.

Therefore all things arise from Tao.
By Virtue they are nourished,
Developed, cared for,
Sheltered, comforted,
Grown, and protected.
Creating without claiming,
Doing without taking credit,
Guiding without interfering,
This is Primal Virtue.

天下有始以為天下母既知其母以知其子既知其子復守其母
沒身不殆塞其兌閉其門終身不勤開其兌濟其事終身不救
見小曰明守柔曰強用其光復歸其明無遺身殃是為習常

FIFTY-TWO

The beginning of the universe
Is the mother of all things.
Knowing the mother, one also knows the sons.
Knowing the sons, yet remaining in touch with the mother,
Brings freedom from the fear of death.

Keep your mouth shut,
Guard the senses,
And life is ever full.
Open your mouth,
Always be busy,
And life is beyond hope.

Seeing the small is insight;
Yielding to force is strength.
Using the outer light, return to insight,
And in this way be saved from harm.
This is learning constancy.

使我介然有知行於大道唯施是畏

大道甚夷而民好徑

朝甚除田甚蕪倉甚虛服文綵帶利劍厭飲食

財貨有餘是謂盜夸非道也哉

FIFTY-THREE

If I have even just a little sense,
I will walk on the main road and my only fear will be of straying from it.
Keeping to the main road is easy,
But people love to be sidetracked.

When the court is arrayed in splendor,
The fields are full of weeds,
And the granaries are bare.
Some wear gorgeous clothes,
Carry sharp swords,
And indulge themselves with food and drink;
They have more possessions than they can use.
They are robber barons.
This is certainly not the way of Tao.

FIFTY-FOUR

What is firmly established cannot be uprooted.
What is firmly grasped cannot slip away.
It will be honored from generation to generation.

Cultivate Virtue in your self,
And Virtue will be real.
Cultivate it in the family,
And Virtue will abound.
Cultivate it in the village,
And Virtue will grow.
Cultivate it in the nation,
And Virtue will be abundant.
Cultivate it in the universe,
And Virtue will be everywhere.

Therefore look at the body as body;
Look at the family as family;
Look at the village as village;
Look at the nation as nation;
Look at the universe as universe.

How do I know the universe is like this?
By looking!

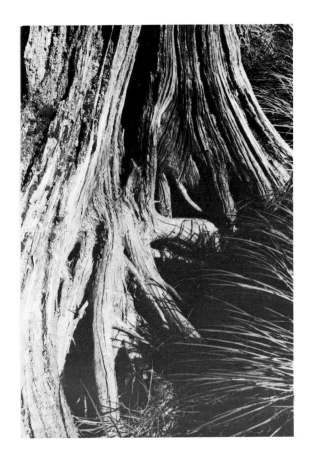

善建者不拔善抱者不脫子孫以祭祀不輟
修之於身其德乃真修之於家其德乃餘
修之於鄉其德乃長修之於國其德乃豐
修之於天下其德乃普
故以身觀身以家觀家以鄉觀鄉以國觀國
以天下觀天下
吾何以知天下然哉以此

FIFTY-FIVE

He who is filled with Virtue is like a newborn child.
Wasps and serpents will not sting him;
Wild beasts will not pounce upon him;
He will not be attacked by birds of prey.
His bones are soft, his muscles weak,
But his grip is firm.
He has not experienced the union of man and woman, but is whole.
His manhood is strong.
He screams all day without becoming hoarse.
This is perfect harmony.

Knowing harmony is constancy.
Knowing constancy is enlightenment.

It is not wise to rush about.
Controlling the breath causes strain.
If too much energy is used, exhaustion follows.
This is not the way of Tao.
Whatever is contrary to Tao will not last long.

含德之厚比於赤子蜂蠆虺蛇不螫猛獸不據攫鳥不搏骨弱筋柔而握固

未知牝牡之合而全作精之至也終日號而不嗄和之至也

知和曰常知常曰明

益生曰祥心使氣曰強物壯則老謂之不道不道早已

知者不言言者不知塞其兌閉其門
挫其銳解其分和其光同其塵
是謂之同
故不可得而親不可得而疏不可得而利
不可得而害不可得而貴不可得而賤
故為天下貴

FIFTY-SIX

Those who know do not talk.
Those who talk do not know.

Keep your mouth closed.
Guard your senses.
Temper your sharpness.
Simplify your problems.
Mask your brightness.
Be at one with the dust of the earth.
This is primal union.

He who has achieved this state
Is unconcerned with friends and enemies,
With good and harm, with honor and disgrace.
This therefore is the highest state of man.

以正治國以奇用兵以無事取天下

吾何以知其然哉以此

天下多忌諱而民彌貧民多利器國家滋昏

人多伎巧奇物滋起法令滋彰盜賊多有

故聖人云我無為而民自化我好靜而民自正

我無事而民自富我無欲而民自樸

## FIFTY-SEVEN

Rule a nation with justice.
Wage war with surprise moves.
Become master of the universe without striving.
How do I know that this is so?
Because of this!

The more laws and restrictions there are,
The poorer people become.
The sharper men's weapons,
The more trouble in the land.
The more ingenious and clever men are,
The more strange things happen.
The more rules and regulations,
The more thieves and robbers.

Therefore the sage says:
    I take no action and people are reformed.
    I enjoy peace and people become honest.
    I do nothing and people become rich.
    I have no desires and people return to the good and simple life.

其政悶悶其民淳淳其政察察其民缺缺
禍兮福之所倚福兮禍之所伏孰知其極其無正
正復為奇善復為妖人之迷其日固久
是以聖人方而不割廉而不劌直而不肆光而不耀

## FIFTY-EIGHT

When the country is ruled with a light hand
The people are simple.
When the country is ruled with severity,
The people are cunning.

Happiness is rooted in misery.
Misery lurks beneath happiness.
Who knows what the future holds?
There is no honesty.
Honesty becomes dishonest.
Goodness becomes witchcraft.
Man's bewitchment lasts for a long time.

Therefore the sage is sharp but not cutting,
Pointed but not piercing,
Straightforward but not unrestrained,
Brilliant but not blinding.

FIFTY-NINE

In caring for others and serving heaven,
There is nothing like using restraint.
Restraint begins with giving up one's own ideas.
This depends on Virtue gathered in the past.
If there is a good store of Virtue, then nothing is impossible.
If nothing is impossible, then there are no limits.
If a man knows no limits, then he is fit to be a ruler.
The mother principle of ruling holds good for a long time.
This is called having deep roots and a firm foundation,
The Tao of long life and eternal vision.

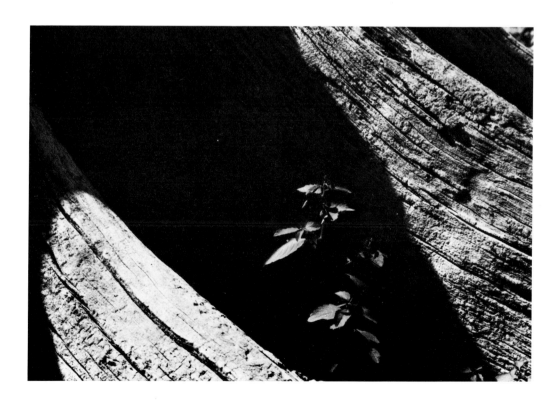

治大國若烹小鮮以道莅天下其鬼不神非其鬼不神

其神不傷人非其神不傷人聖人亦不傷人

夫兩不相傷故德交歸焉

SIXTY

Ruling the country is like cooking a small fish.
Approach the universe with Tao,
And evil will have no power.
Not that evil is not powerful,
But its power will not be used to harm others.
Not only will it do no harm to others,
But the sage himself will also be protected.
They do not hurt each other,
And the Virtue in each one refreshes both.

大國者下流，天下之交，天下之牝。

牝常以靜勝牡，以靜為下。

故大國以下小國，則取小國；小國以下大國，則取大國。故或下以取，或下而取。

大國不過欲兼畜人，小國不過欲入事人。

夫兩者各得其所欲，大者宜為下。

SIXTY-ONE

A great country is like low land.
It is the meeting ground of the universe,
The mother of the universe.

The female overcomes the male with stillness,
Lying low in stillness.

Therefore if a great country gives way to a smaller country,
It will conquer the smaller country.
And if a small country submits to a great country,
It can conquer the great country.
Therefore those who would conquer must yield,
And those who conquer do so because they yield.

A great nation needs more people;
A small country needs to serve.
Each gets what it wants.
It is fitting for a great nation to yield.

SIXTY-TWO

Tao is the source of the ten thousand things.
It is the treasure of the good man, and the refuge of the bad.
Sweet words can buy honor;
Good deeds can gain respect.
If a man is bad, do not abandon him.
Therefore on the day the emperor is crowned,
Or the three officers of state installed,
Do not send a gift of jade and a team of four horses,
But remain still and offer the Tao.
Why does everyone like the Tao so much at first?
Isn't it because you find what you seek and are forgiven when you sin?
Therefore this is the greatest treasure of the universe.

道者万物之奥善人之宝不善人之所保
美言可以市尊行可以加人人之不善何棄之有
故立天子置三公雖有拱璧以先駟馬不如坐進此道
古之所以貴此道者何不曰以求得有罪以免邪故為天下貴

SIXTY-THREE

Practice non-action.
Work without doing.
Taste the tasteless.
Magnify the small, increase the few.
Reward bitterness with care.

See simplicity in the complicated.
Achieve greatness in little things.

In the universe the difficult things are done as if they are easy.
In the universe great acts are made up of small deeds.
The sage does not attempt anything very big,
And thus achieves greatness.

Easy promises make for little trust.
Taking things lightly results in great difficulty.
Because the sage always confronts difficulties,
He never experiences them.

為無為事無事味無味大小多少報怨以德
圖難於其易為大於其細天下難事必作於易
天下大事必作於細是以聖人終不為大故能成其大
夫輕諾必寡信多易必多難是以聖人猶難之
故終無難矣

夫安易持，其未兆易謀，其脆易泮，其微易散。為之於未有，治之於未亂。

合抱之木生於毫末，九層之臺起於累土，千里之行始於足下。

為者敗之，執者失之，以聖人無為故無敗，無執故無失。

民之從事常於幾成而敗之，慎終如始則無敗事。

是以聖人欲不欲，不貴難得之貨，學不學，復眾人之所過，

以輔萬物之自然而不敢為。

## SIXTY-FOUR

Peace is easily maintained;
Trouble is easily overcome before it starts.
The brittle is easily shattered;
The small is easily scattered.

Deal with it before it happens.
Set things in order before there is confusion.

A tree as great as a man's embrace springs from a small shoot;
A terrace nine stories high begins with a pile of earth;
A journey of a thousand miles starts under one's feet.

He who acts defeats his own purpose;
He who grasps loses.
The sage does not act, and so is not defeated.
He does not grasp and therefore does not lose.

People usually fail when they are on the verge of success.
So give as much care to the end as to the beginning;
Then there will be no failure.

Therefore the sage seeks freedom from desire.
He does not collect precious things.
He learns not to hold on to ideas.
He brings men back to what they have lost.
He helps the ten thousand things find their own nature,
But refrains from action.

SIXTY-FIVE

In the beginning those who knew the Tao did not try to enlighten others,
But kept them in the dark.
Why is it so hard to rule?
Because people are so clever.
Rulers who try to use cleverness
Cheat the country.
Those who rule without cleverness
Are a blessing to the land.
These are the two alternatives.
Understanding these is Primal Virtue.
Primal Virtue is deep and far.
It leads all things back
Toward the great oneness.

古之善為道者非以明民將以愚之民之難治以其智多
故以智治國國之賊不以智治國國之福
知此兩者亦稽式常知稽式是謂玄德
玄德深矣遠矣與物反矣然後乃至大順

江海所以能為百谷王者以其善下之故能為百谷王

是以欲上民必以言下之欲先民必以身後之

是以聖人處上而民不重處前而民不害

是以天下樂推而不厭以其不爭故天下莫能與之爭

SIXTY-SIX

Why is the sea king of a hundred streams?
Because it lies below them.
Therefore it is the king of a hundred streams.

If the sage would guide the people, he must serve with humility.
If he would lead them, he must follow behind.
In this way when the sage rules, the people will not feel oppressed;
When he stands before them, they will not be harmed.
The whole world will support him and will not tire of him.

Because he does not compete,
He does not meet competition.

SIXTY-SEVEN

Everyone under heaven says that my Tao is great and beyond compare.
Because it is great, it seems different.
If it were not different, it would have vanished long ago.

I have three treasures which I hold and keep.
The first is mercy; the second is economy;
The third is daring not to be ahead of others.
From mercy comes courage; from economy comes generosity;
From humility comes leadership.

Nowadays men shun mercy, but try to be brave;
They abandon economy, but try to be generous;
They do not believe in humility, but always try to be first.
This is certain death.

Mercy brings victory in battle and strength in defense.
It is the means by which heaven saves and guards.

天下皆知美之為美，斯惡已；皆知善之為善，斯不善已。故有無相生，難易相成，長短相形，高下相盈，音聲相和，前後相隨，恆也。是以聖人處無為之事，行不言之教；萬物作而弗始，生而弗有，為而弗恃，功成而弗居。夫唯弗居，是以不去。

善為士者不武，善戰者不怒，善勝敵者不與，善用人者為之下，是謂不爭之德，是謂用人之力，是謂配天古之極

SIXTY-EIGHT

A good soldier is not violent.
A good fighter is not angry.
A good winner is not vengeful.
A good employer is humble.
This is known as the Virtue of not striving.
This is known as ability to deal with people.
This since ancient times has been known
    as the ultimate unity with heaven.

用兵有言吾不敢為主而為客不敢進寸而退尺
是謂行無行攘無臂扔無敵執無兵
禍莫大於輕敵輕敵幾喪吾寶故抗兵相加哀者勝矣

## SIXTY-NINE

There is a saying among soldiers:
    I dare not make the first move but would rather play the guest;
    I dare not advance an inch but would rather withdraw a foot.

This is called marching without appearing to move,
Rolling up your sleeves without showing your arm,
Capturing the enemy without attacking,
Being armed without weapons.

There is no greater catastrophe than underestimating the enemy.
By underestimating the enemy, I almost lose what I value.

Therefore when the battle is joined,
The underdog will win.

SEVENTY

My words are easy to understand and easy to perform,
Yet no man under heaven knows them or practices them.

My words have ancient beginnings.
My actions are disciplined.
Because men do not understand, they have no knowledge of me.

Those that know me are few;
Those that abuse me are honored.
Therefore the sage wears rough clothing and holds the jewel in his heart.

吾言甚易知甚易行天下莫能知莫能行
言有宗事有君夫唯無知是以不我知
知我者希則我者貴是以聖人被褐懷玉

SEVENTY-ONE

Knowing ignorance is strength.
Ignoring knowledge is sickness.

If one is sick of sickness, then one is not sick.
The sage is not sick because he is sick of sickness.
Therefore he is not sick.

知不知上不知知病夫唯病病是以不病聖人不病以其病病是以不病

民不畏威則大威至
無狎其所居無厭其所生夫唯不厭是以不厭
是以聖人自知不自見自愛不自貴故去彼取此

SEVENTY-TWO

When men lack a sense of awe, there will be disaster.

Do not intrude in their homes.
Do not harass them at work.
If you do not interfere, they will not weary of you.

Therefore the sage knows himself but makes no show,
Has self-respect but is not arrogant.
He lets go of that and chooses this.

## SEVENTY-THREE

A brave and passionate man will kill or be killed.
A brave and calm man will always preserve life.
Of these two which is good and which is harmful?
Some things are not favored by heaven. Who knows why?
Even the sage is unsure of this.

The Tao of heaven does not strive, and yet it overcomes.
It does not speak, and yet is answered.
It does not ask, yet is supplied with all its needs.
It seems at ease, and yet it follows a plan.

Heaven's net casts wide.
Though its meshes are coarse, nothing slips through.

勇於敢則殺勇於不敢則活此兩者或利或害

天之所惡孰知其故是以聖人猶難之

天之道不爭而善勝不言而善應不召而自來

繟然而善謀天網恢恢疏而不失

民不畏死奈何以死懼之
若使民常畏死而為奇者吾得執而殺之孰敢
常有司殺者殺夫代司殺者殺是謂代大匠斲
夫代大匠斲者希有不傷其手矣

## SEVENTY-FOUR

If men are not afraid to die,
It is of no avail to threaten them with death.

If men live in constant fear of dying,
And if breaking the law means that a man will be killed,
Who will dare to break the law?

There is always an official executioner.
If you try to take his place,
It is like trying to be a master carpenter and cutting wood.
If you try to cut wood like a master carpenter,
    you will only hurt your hand.

民之饑以其上食稅之多是以饑民之難治以其上之有為是以難治民之輕死以其上求生之厚是以輕死夫唯無以生為者是賢於貴生

SEVENTY-FIVE

Why are the people starving?
Because the rulers eat up the money in taxes.
Therefore the people are starving.

Why are the people rebellious?
Because the rulers interfere too much.
Therefore they are rebellious.

Why do the people think so little of death?
Because the rulers demand too much of life.
Therefore the people take death lightly.

Having little to live on, one knows better than to value life too much.

人之生也柔弱其死也堅強萬物草木之生也柔脆
其死也枯槁故堅強者死之徒柔弱者生之徒
是以兵強則不勝木強則兵強大處下柔弱處上

SEVENTY-SIX

A man is born gentle and weak.
At his death he is hard and stiff.
Green plants are tender and filled with sap.
At their death they are withered and dry.

Therefore the stiff and unbending is the disciple of death.
The gentle and yielding is the disciple of life.

Thus an army without flexibility never wins a battle.
A tree that is unbending is easily broken.

The hard and strong will fall.
The soft and weak will overcome.

## SEVENTY-SEVEN

The Tao of heaven is like the bending of a bow.
The high is lowered, and the low is raised.
If the string is too long, it is shortened;
If there is not enough, it is made longer.

The Tao of heaven is to take from those who have too much
    and give to those who do not have enough.
Man's way is different.
He takes from those who do not have enough
    to give to those who already have too much.
What man has more than enough and gives it to the world?
Only the man of Tao.

Therefore the sage works without recognition.
He achieves what has to be done without dwelling on it.
He does not try to show his knowledge.

天之道夫猶張弓與高者抑之下者舉之

有餘者損之不足者補之

天之道損有餘而補不足之人之道則不然損不足以奉有餘

孰能有餘以奉天下唯有道者

是以聖人為而不恃功成而不處其不欲見賢

天下莫柔弱於水而攻堅強者莫之能勝以其無以易之

弱之勝強柔之勝剛天下莫不知莫能行

是以聖人云受國之垢是謂社稷主受國不祥

是為天下王正言若反

## SEVENTY-EIGHT

Under heaven nothing is more soft and yielding than water.
Yet for attacking the solid and strong, nothing is better;
It has no equal.
The weak can overcome the strong;
The supple can overcome the stiff.
Under heaven everyone knows this,
Yet no one puts it into practice.
Therefore the sage says:
    He who takes upon himself the humiliation of the people
        is fit to rule them.
    He who takes upon himself the country's disasters deserves
        to be king of the universe.
The truth often sounds paradoxical.

和大怨必有餘怨安可以為善是以聖人執左契

而不責於人有德司契無德司徹

天道無親常與善人

## SEVENTY-NINE

After a bitter quarrel, some resentment must remain.
What can one do about it?
Therefore the sage keeps his half of the bargain
But does not exact his due.
A man of Virtue performs his part,
But a man without Virtue requires others to fulfill their obligations.
The Tao of heaven is impartial.
It stays with good men all the time.

小國寡民使有什伯之器而不用
使民重死而不遠徙雖有舟輿無所乘之
雖有甲兵無所陳之使人復結繩而用之
甘其食美其服安其居樂其俗
鄰國相望雞犬之聲相聞
民至老死不相往来

EIGHTY

A small country has fewer people.
Though there are machines that can work ten to a hundred times faster
        than man, they are not needed.
The people take death seriously and do not travel far.
Though they have boats and carriages, no one uses them.
Though they have armor and weapons, no one displays them.
Men return to the knotting of rope in place of writing.
Their food is plain and good, their clothes fine but simple,
        their homes secure;
They are happy in their ways.
Though they live within sight of their neighbors,
And crowing cocks and barking dogs are heard across the way,
Yet they leave each other in peace while they grow old and die.

信言不美美言不信善者不辯辯者不善知者不博博者不知

聖人不積既以為人己愈有既以與人己愈多

天之道利而不害聖人之道為而不爭

## EIGHTY-ONE

Truthful words are not beautiful.
Beautiful words are not truthful.
Good men do not argue.
Those who argue are not good.
Those who know are not learned.
The learned do not know.

The sage never tries to store things up.
The more he does for others, the more he has.
The more he gives to others, the greater his abundance.
The Tao of heaven is pointed but does no harm.
The Tao of the sage is work without effort.

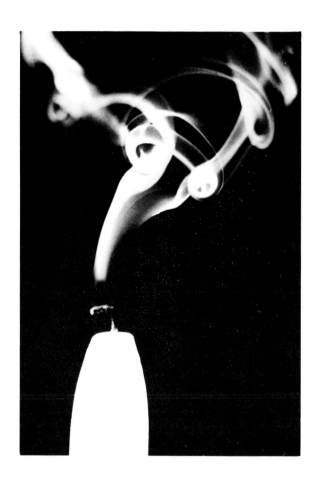

A NOTE ABOUT THE TRANSLATORS

Gia-fu Feng was born in Shanghai in 1919, was educated
in China, and came to the United States in 1947 to study
comparative religion. He holds a BA from Peking
University and an MA from the University of
Pennsylvania. He has taught at the Esalen Institute,
Big Sur, and now directs the Stillpoint Foundation, a
Taoist meditation center in Colorado. He is the author
(with Jerome Kirk) of *Tai Chi—A Way of Centering—
& I Ching*, which was published in 1970.

Jane English, whose photographs form an integral part of
this book, holds an BA from Mount Holyoke College
and has received a doctorate from the University of
Wisconsin for her work in high energy particle physics.
She is at the moment teaching a course in Oriental
thought and modern physics at Colorado College (with
Gia-fu Feng as guest lecturer). She was born in Boston,
Massachusetts, in 1942.

A NOTE ON THE TYPE

This book was set on the Monotype in Centaur, a type
face designed by Bruce Rogers (1870–1957) and adapted
by him for machine composition in 1929. It is the only
type face designed by Rogers that is available for machine
typesetting. The letter forms are based on the type face
used by the Venetian printer Nicholas Jenson for his
edition of Eusebius in 1470. Centaur is lighter in color
than the Jenson type and has sharper serifs, but it
preserves both the generously wide letter forms and
strong sense of the calligraphic tradition that characterize
the Venetian type faces of the fifteenth century.

Typography and binding design by Clint Anglin.